SHOW ME HOW
I Can Grow Things

Gardening projects for kids
shown step by step

SALLY WALTON & STEPHANIE DONALDSON

This edition is published by Armadillo,
an imprint of Anness Publishing Ltd, Blaby Road,
Wigston, Leicestershire LE18 4SE; info@anness.com

www.annesspublishing.com

If you like the images in this book and would like to
investigate using them for publishing, promotions or
advertising, please visit our website www.practicalpictures.com
for more information.

Publisher: Joanna Lorenz
Project Editors: Judith Simons and Richard McGinlay
Additional projects by Jenny Hendy
Designers: Peter Butler and Edward Kinsey
Photographers: John Freeman with Howard Rice
Production Controller: Pirong Wang

ACKNOWLEDGEMENTS
The publishers would like to thank the following children
for appearing in this book, and of course their parents:
Josie and Laurie Ainscough, Rosie Anness, Rebecca Clee,
Reece Harle, Dominic Henry, Jock Maitland, Ilaira and
Joshua Mallalieu, Alexander Martin-Simons, Tania Murphy,
Alexander and Dominic Paneth, Brandon Rayment, Grace
and Matthew Royale, and Roxy Walton.

PUBLISHER'S NOTE
The level of adult supervision needed will depend on the
abilities and age of the children following the projects.
However, we advise that adult supervision is always
preferable, and vital if the project calls for the use of sharp
knives or other utensils, and fertilizers/plant food.
Each project clearly states when adult supervision is obviously
called for. Always keep potentially harmful gardening tools
and products well out of the reach of young children.
Although the advice and information in this book are believed
to be accurate and true at the time of going to press, neither
the authors nor the publisher can accept any legal
responsibility or liability for any errors or omissions that may
have been made nor for any inaccuracies nor for any loss,
harm or injury that comes about from following instructions
or advice in this book.

Manufacturer: Anness Publishing Ltd, Blaby Road,
Wigston, Leicestershire LE18 4SE, England
For Product Tracking go to:
www.annesspublishing.com/tracking
Batch: 1416-22468-1127

Contents

Introduction

Gardens and gardeners come in many shapes and sizes. You can be a gardener too, whether you live on a farm with a large garden or in an apartment with some space on a windowsill for a few plants.

Growing things takes time and patience, but the rewards are worth waiting for. There are lots of other things for you to be getting on with while your seeds are germinating under the soil. Once you see the first green shoots appear you will know that a plant really is going to grow and you are already a gardener!

Birdseed surprises

In this chapter we show you how to grow lots of different plants yourself, with perhaps just a little help from a grown-up. There are plants that grow very fast and produce something to eat, like mustard and cress. Some plants take longer to grow but give you special treats, like strawberries. Other plants are grown just for fun, like vegetable tops and a coconut head. So, whether you choose to grow giant sunflowers that take all summer, or sprouting seeds for your salad that are ready in just a few days, you will find out all you need to know by following what the children are doing in the pictures.

Different plants grow, then flower and die with the seasons.

Strawberries

Vegetable tops

Daffodils like the crisp, cold springtime sunshine while nasturtiums thrive in the baking hot summer sun, needing no shade and very little water. Some plants live through the winter, growing new flowers each summer. Others live only for one season but make seeds that will grow into new plants the following year. Houseplants usually come from parts of the world where the weather is warmer all year round, but they grow very happily indoors in countries with cooler climates.

How Plants Begin to Grow

Plants start growing in many different ways and it is important to know how to treat each type. Look at the list below to find out how plants can be grown.

Seeds

A seed needs water to soften its outer shell, and then the new plant sends a root downwards into the soil and a stem upwards, towards the light. The tiniest seeds just need to be sprinkled on top of the soil, but the larger ones have to be buried. Usually seeds are planted as deep as they are thick. So measure a seed between your fingers and you will know how deep it has to go into the soil in order to grow properly.

Seeds

Bulbs, corms and tubers

Bulbs

Tubers

Corms

These are thick, fleshy and roundish in shape. A bulb looks like an onion – in fact if you planted an onion it would grow leaves and flowers! They all produce new plants which will grow in the right conditions. Some need icy cold winters underground and others should only be planted when the weather gets warmer. Daffodils grow from bulbs, begonias from corms and dahlias from tubers.

Grow a new plant from a stem cutting

Cuttings

Some plants need very special conditions to make their seeds grow, but you can still grow some new plants from cuttings. Take a piece of the healthy full-grown plant, and stand it in water or compost (soil mix) in a warm place. It will grow roots from its stem and you will soon have a strong little plant. Some plants can be grown from leaf or root cuttings as well.

Plantlets

Some fully-grown plants send out long runners which grow miniature plants at their ends. These send down roots of their own if they rest on the soil, and eventually the runners will die back to leave a separate new plant. Strawberries and spider plants grow in this way.

Grow a new plant from plantlets

Caring for Your Plants

Your seeds, bulbs, cuttings and plantlets will only grow into healthy adult plants if you look after them carefully. This doesn't need to take a lot of time, but you do need to remember to look at them every few days to check that they are doing well.

Watering

Giving your plants a drink is a lot of fun, but if you give them too much they will rot and die. Try to keep the soil damp but not wet. When you press it with your finger, you should be able to feel the moisture without a little pool of water forming. If your plants do dry out, stand their pots in a saucer or bowl of water rather than pour on water from above. This way the soil will gradually soak up water to feed the thirsty roots.

Test the soil to see if it needs more water

If the soil is dry, stand the pot in a bowl of water

Weeds

If you do your gardening outdoors, you may find that other little plants also begin to grow where you haven't planted any seeds. Ask a grown-up to show you what weeds look like, and try to keep your garden weed-free. It seems cruel to pull out healthy little plants, but if you leave them they will spread very quickly and stop your plants from getting the light and moisture that they need to grow. So pull them up before they grow big enough to flower and make more seeds to grow more weeds.

Pests

These are creatures that we don't want around us, and in the garden they include aphids, caterpillars, snails and slugs. They love eating juicy new plants but luckily there are some other creatures that like eating them. Ladybirds (ladybugs) love aphids, but they can't always eat them up quickly enough so you may have to do something. Try adding a small amount of washing-up soap (dishwashing detergent) to a spray bottle filled with water and use it to spray the aphids on your plants. If you have a problem with slugs and snails, you can sprinkle ashes or sand around your lettuces as they don't like the feeling of sliding over it. Caterpillars need to be removed by hand and – if you don't mind doing it – just drop them into a jar of water. Otherwise, set them free somewhere far away from your precious plants.

Spray a plant with soapy water to get rid of aphids

Important!

Remember that even the most expert gardeners sometimes have failures, when plants don't grow, or pests become a big problem. If this happens to you, try not to feel discouraged. The best thing to do is to try something new so that you always have some gardening on the go!

Latin Names

Every plant has a special Latin name that tells you exactly what it is. Just like we have our Christian names and surnames, a plant has a family name first and its own name second. The names are often difficult to say, but if you take a few letters at a time you will be able to join them up and say something in Latin. When they are printed in a book, Latin names appear in italics, like this: *Helianthus debilis. Helianthus* is the family name for sunflowers, and *debilis* is the special name given to a small, or dwarf, type of sunflower.

Glossary

Here are some special gardening words that you may not know but will see mentioned in the projects.

Alpine A rock garden plant.
Annual A plant that completes its life cycle in one year. It starts by growing from a seed and finishes by making new seeds.
Compost (soil mix) A special soil mixture or rotted-down garden and kitchen waste that feeds the plants so that they can grow well.
Crocks Broken pieces of clay flowerpot. They are used in the bottom of pots to help with drainage.
Cutting A piece of plant (leaf, stem or root) which can be used to grow a new plant.
Germination The first stage of growth from seed to plant.
Node A stem joint, where new stems and leaves grow.
Mulch A layer of chopped up leaves, bark or other plant matter. It is spread on top of the soil to stop it drying out and to prevent weeds from growing.
Propagating Growing new plants by different methods, including taking cuttings.
Runner A creeping stem which grows roots and produces new plants.

Mulches stop the soil drying out so quickly

New umbrella plants are grown from cuttings

Spider plants grow runners

Finding What You Need

Gardening suppliers can be very large and confusing when you only need a few small things to start you off. Here is a basic list of useful gardening materials and tools. You will be able to get some of the equipment mentioned here from toy stores, too, such as a small plastic watering can, a scoop to use as a trowel and a sieve, which are often sold for playing with in sandpits.

Trowel You will need a small trowel for filling flowerpots with compost and for digging holes in the garden.
Watering can A can with a sprinkler will be best for gentle watering. Remember that water is very heavy to carry, so choose the size of can that you will be able to lift easily when it is full.
Sieve This is useful for sprinkling a very fine layer of compost over your newly-sown seeds.
Flowerpots These should always have

a drainage hole in the bottom. They come in lots of different sizes, made from either clay or plastic, and they usually have matching saucers to stop drips. You can decorate clay pots at home or buy plastic ones in lots of fun shades. Don't forget to collect some pretty outer containers too. Clay pots need a layer of crocks or pebbles adding to them before the compost. This helps them to drain better after watering.

Peat pots These are special types of flowerpots which are usually used for planting seeds. When the new plant has started to grow the plant and its pot can be planted in a larger flowerpot. The peat pot will gradually dissolve in the compost.

Seed trays These are useful for planting lots of little seeds or for standing pots of seeds in. You can also use foil dishes used for freezing food.

Seed tray

Plastic flowerpots

Foil dish

Plant labels

Watering can

Plant food

Pen

Hairpins

Compost (soil mix)

Peat pots

Sieve

Plastic bags

Compost (soil mix) Specially prepared soils that we buy in bags are called composts. There are lots of different mixtures that suit some types of plant better than others. Seed and cutting compost will give you the best chance of success with new plants. Houseplant compost is useful for indoor gardeners. Cactus compost is good for succulents. Any all-purpose compost (soil mix) is good for general growing, and it comes in bags of all sizes.

Plant food Some plants need more "food" than they can get from compost alone while they are growing. Always ask a grown-up to help you measure out the correct amount of special plant food, following the instructions on the bottle or packet.

Crocks and pebbles These are used to provide better drainage in the bottom of clay pots. You can also sprinkle a layer of pebbles or gravel on top of the compost. This both looks nice and is good for the plants as it helps to keep the soil moist.

Canes and string Some plants grow tall and their stems need to be supported to stop them bending or breaking.

Hairpins These are used to pin baby plantlets growing on the end of runners into compost so that they form roots.

Plant labels and pen Always label your plants so you can remember what you are growing in different pots.

Seeds, bulbs etc There are usually more than you need in a packet, so before buying any ask grown-up gardeners, like your parents, grandparents or neighbours, whether they can spare you a few of their left-over seeds or bulbs. Gardeners always like to share things.

Plastic flowerpots

Plant containers

Trowels

Watering can

Safety scissors

Pebbles

Crocks

String

Canes

Seeds and bulbs

A Sunflower Race

You have to look up to see a sunflower, because they are the tallest and the biggest flowers that we grow in our gardens. It's great fun to have a sunflower race with your friends or family. Roxy and Dominic are having a sunflower race. Follow the step-by-step photographs to see who won.

Tasty pickings

The heads of sunflowers are sometimes as large as dinner plates and packed with tasty seeds. These seeds can be eaten raw once the husks have been removed, or the whole flowerhead can be dried and hung out to feed the birds in winter. In hot countries you can sometimes see whole fields of huge sunflowers that are grown to make cooking oil and margarine.

YOU WILL NEED THESE MATERIALS AND TOOLS

Small flowerpots

All-purpose compost (soil mix)

Trowel

Sunflower seeds

Plant labels

Watering can

Liquid plant food

Large flowerpots

Long bamboo canes

1 Fill some pots with compost (soil mix) and press in the seeds.

2 Water the pots and cover them with black plastic, or put them in a dark place to germinate.

Size is Not Everything

If you really love sunflowers but have no space to grow the very tall ones, don't worry – you can grow the smaller types. Buy a packet of sunflower seed called *Helianthus debilis.* Sow the seeds into peat pots and then move them into medium-sized flowerpots or a space in the garden, if you have one. They will grow about 80cm (2ft 8in) tall, and are just as beautiful.

3 When the seeds germinate and you can see a bit of green, move the pots into the light.

4 When the seedlings are big enough to handle, they can be moved into bigger pots. To help them grow strong and tall you will need to give them a liquid feed once a week. Ask a grown-up to help you with this.

Above: As the plants grow you will need to move them into even larger pots or plant them in the garden. They will need canes to support them.

Some of the plants will be bigger than you are. Measure each one to find the winner of the great sunflower race. This one is a dead heat!

Juicy Strawberries

Strawberry plants have very pretty pink or white flowers with yellow middles, and when the petals drop the fruits begin to grow. They are green at first and then white. As they get bigger and juicier, and ripen in the sun they gradually turn a shiny bright red. If you can bear to wait you will find that the riper they get, the sweeter they taste.

How do baby strawberry plants grow?

Strawberry plants send out long thin stems called runners and baby plants form at their ends. They are fed by the root system of the parent plant through the runner. But if these babies come to rest on soil, they put down roots of their own and no longer need the parent plant to keep them alive. Tania is going to start off some baby strawberry plants and grow herself a mouthwatering treat.

Below: Delicious juicy strawberries – well worth waiting for.

YOU WILL NEED THESE MATERIALS AND TOOLS

Small flowerpots and saucers

Trowel

Potting compost (soil mix)

Strawberry plant with runners

Hairpin for each baby plant

Watering can

Safety scissors

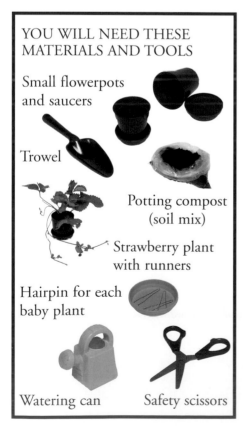

14

Cascading Strawberries

If you only have a small space for growing your fruits, a strawberry pot is useful and pretty. It is a tall pot with little "balconies" all the way around it. The idea is to fill the whole pot with compost and plant a small strawberry baby in each of the openings. Water each one and plant the biggest strawberry plant in the top of the pot. When the plants begin to grow they will cover the pot and strawberries will hang down in the sun to ripen.

1 Fill the small flowerpots with potting compost (soil mix) and gently firm it down.

2 Place your pots around the parent plant so that a baby plant rests in each of the pots. Push a hairpin into the compost over the runner.

3 Water all the pots. Remember to check the compost each day to be sure it never gets too dry.

4 When the plants have rooted you will see tiny new leaves beginning to sprout.

5 If the baby strawberry plants feel firm in the compost, you can now cut the runners.

6 As your plant grows it will need more space, either in the garden or a larger pot.

7 Remember to water your strawberry plant regularly. If it's kept too dry, the fruit will shrivel.

Coconut Head

This coconut head looks so funny that you'll have to be careful who you show it to – everyone will want one! They are so easy to do, and as the grass grows you will be able to change the hair-style of your coconut head. You could also try sowing mustard and cress for a really curly hair-style. Follow the method shown by Dominic and Alex.

Nuts about hair

You can buy grass seed in small amounts from most hardware stores or gardening suppliers, and just 50g (2oz) will grow a really good "head of hair" for your coconut. You will have to ask a grown-up to saw or break the top off your coconut, because the shells are really hard. If you haven't eaten fresh coconut before or drunk coconut milk, try some – it's really tasty! Put some out for the birds as a treat.

YOU WILL NEED THESE MATERIALS AND TOOLS

Fresh coconut

Flowerpot

Marker pen

Trowel

Compost (soil mix)

Grass seed

Soil sieve

Watering can

Black plastic bag

1 Ask a grown-up to take the top off your coconut. Pour out the milk and ask someone to help you remove the flesh – it's quite difficult.

2 Stand the coconut shell in a flower-pot to stop it falling over, and draw a face on it with a chunky marker pen.

3 Fill your coconut with compost (soil mix), pressing it down gently.

4 Sprinkle grass seed thickly over the top of the compost.

5 Sieve a thin layer of compost over to cover all the seed. Press down gently again.

6 Water and cover with a black plastic bag, or put in a dark place until the seeds have begun to grow.

7 When green shoots appear, stand the coconut in the light and water when it looks dry. When the grass has grown over the rim of the coconut, it is ready for its first haircut.

Above: Before and after! If you keep snipping the grass as it grows, it will get thicker and thicker!

Tumbling Tradescantia

These creeping plants are wonderfully easy to propagate from cuttings. They have attractive, variegated leaves and pretty names to match them, such as inch plant, purple heart and teddy bear vine. Follow what Brandon is doing and grow a lovely plant which you could give to someone on their birthday.

Encouraging growth

Tradescantia live happily indoors as long as they have light, warmth and a small amount of water. They don't mind at all if you break a bit off to start a new plant. In fact it encourages them to sprout more stems and become even bushier. When your new plant is growing well, pinch off the tips of the stems and watch it grow bigger and bigger.

Below: If you keep your new plants in a light place and water them when they get dry, they will soon start to grow well.

YOU WILL NEED THESE
MATERIALS AND TOOLS

Tradescantia

Glass of water

Small flowerpot and saucer

Houseplant
compost (soil
mix)

Trowel

Watering can

1 Break off three leafy stems from the parent plant.

2 Carefully peel off the lower leaves from your cuttings.

3 Place the cuttings in the glass of water, so that just the stem is in the water.

4 After three or four days you will be able to see small roots forming. When they are as long as your little finger the new plants are ready to be potted in soil.

5 Hold the plants in a small pot and sprinkle the compost (soil mix) around them until their roots are fully covered. Ask a grown-up to help you do this if you find it difficult.

Minty Options

You can grow mint in the same way as tradescantia. Just take a strong, healthy stem from a mint plant, remove the lower leaves and stand it in a glass of water in a sunny place. Within a week you will be able to see lots of roots forming on the lower stem. Pot this up in compost or, if you have a garden, choose a damp spot in which to plant it. Mint likes a lot of water.

6 Carefully firm the compost around the plants, filling the pot to within 3cm (1in) of the top.

7 Water your plants so the compost is moist and they will grow. Stand the pot on a light, but not too sunny, windowsill.

Surprise Plants

Do you like spicy, Eastern or African food? Or do your parents cook it? If so, you probably have sweet potatoes (sometimes called yams) and fresh root ginger in your kitchen. Did you know you can grow plants from them? Follow what Laurie and Josie are doing on the next page and you'll see how it's done.

A taste of Asia

Fresh ginger root is an important ingredient in Asian and Chinese cooking. The root is dried and powdered too, and we use it in desserts, cakes and gingersnaps. You can grow a ginger plant from a piece of the fresh root. Sweet potatoes look pinker than potatoes, and taste much sweeter. They grow in Africa, and North and South America, where they are very popular. A sweet potato can be planted whole, and it will grow into a twining houseplant with sweet-smelling flowers.

Below: Everyone will be curious to know the names of these unusual plants – sweet potato (left) and ginger (right).

YOU WILL NEED THESE
MATERIALS AND TOOLS

Piece of ginger
root, with
growing buds

Two flowerpots

Trowel

Compost
(soil mix)

Watering can

Plastic bag
and fastener

Gravel

Sweet potato

Surprise Plants from the Kitchen

There are all sorts of fruit and vegetables that have seeds you could grow. An avocado has a really big stone (pit) that will germinate if you rest half of it in water. Rest it in a jar using cocktail sticks or toothpicks, so that the flat end is in water, and put it in a light place. It may take a while, but the stone will split and send down a root. Pot it in compost and you will soon have a small tree with big glossy green leaves. A spikey pineapple top, stood in water, will grow roots. If you pot it in compost and keep it warm, it will grow a new spikey top. It would have to be very warm for a long time to grow fruit. Why don't you try growing passion fruit seeds, orange and lemon seeds, even date pits. The hard seeds will need to be cracked to help them germinate.

1 Cut off a 5cm (2in) piece of ginger root making sure that it has good growing buds.

2 Fill a pot with compost (soil mix), and press the root into the surface so that the buds just peep out.

3 Water the pot and place it inside a plastic bag in a warm dark place.

4 When the leaves begin to sprout, open the plastic bag. Spread some gravel on top of the compost and stand on a warm, sunny windowsill.

5 To grow the sweet potato, half fill a deep pot with compost, and rest the tuber on the surface.

6 Fill the pot with more compost, so that the tuber is completely covered with a thick layer of compost. Water well, and seal it in a plastic bag. Put it in a warm, dark place.

7 It will take about 14 days to start growing. As soon as the first leaves start showing, take off the bag and move it into the light. It will grow very fast. Twine its stem around a cane.

Desert Bowl

Succulent plants come from very dry countries where there is hardly any rain at all. Succulent means juicy or filled with sap. To stay alive these clever plants use their roots to suck up any moisture that is in the sandy soil, and they store it in their thick stems or leaves. Try planting up a container with five different types of succulent plants like Joshua and Ilaira have done, and create your own desert environment.

Propagating succulents

Baby plants form on the edges of leaves or on the sides of stems and these can be planted in their own small flower-pots. Succulent plants that you have grown like this make nice presents, and because they grow on indoor windowsills, they suit everyone.

Some succulent plants – known as cacti – are spikey, or covered with fine hairs that sting if you get them in your fingers. Avoid the ones that can hurt you because there are many more safe succulents to choose from.

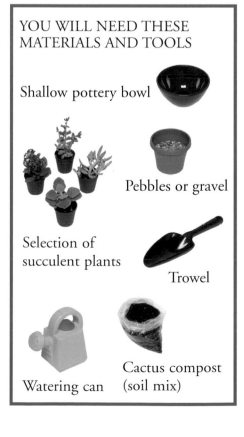

YOU WILL NEED THESE
MATERIALS AND TOOLS

Shallow pottery bowl

Pebbles or gravel

Selection of
succulent plants

Trowel

Watering can

Cactus compost
(soil mix)

Alpine Garden

There is another sort of tiny garden you can grow in a pottery dish or shallow round flowerpot. An alpine garden needs gritty soil and pebbles for good drainage. A pet store will sell small bags of gravel or grit because it is used in fish tanks. Mix equal quantities of grit and compost and put at least five little alpine plants in your dish. Most gardening stockists have a special area for alpine plants, and there are plenty to choose from.

1 Fill the bottom of the bowl with a 5cm (2in) layer of gravel.

2 Before you plant your garden, plan where the plants will look best by placing them in the bowl and moving them around in their individual pots.

3 Remove each plant from its pot very carefully. Take your time, as succulents are brittle and bits fall off quite easily.

4 When all the plants are in the bowl, fill all the spaces around the roots with cactus compost (soil mix), and gently firm the plants in place.

5 Give the plants a little drink, but not too much. Remember that succulents live in sandy places and deserts, and hate to have wet roots.

6 To finish your succulent garden, spread gravel over the surface.

Right: Keep your desert bowl on a sunny windowsill – succulents love the warmth and light.

Safari Garden

This indoor garden creates an exciting setting for your zoo animals. All the plants and the pool fit into a waterproof tray, which can be placed on a tabletop close to a window. Water very sparingly when the compost looks a little dry and mist with a sprayer.

YOU WILL NEED THESE MATERIALS AND TOOLS

Houseplant compost (soil mix)
Waterproof container, such as
  a sterilized cat litter tray trowel
Aluminium foil
Bucket of water
Ribbon plant or lucky bamboo
  (*Dracaena sanderiana*)
Delta maidenhair or maidenhair
  fern (*Adiantum raddianum*)
Shallow dish of water
Bead plant (*Nertera granadensis*)
Dragon tree or pineapple plant
  (*Dracaena* 'Janet Craig
  Compacta')
Pink quill or
  air plant
  (*Tillandsia
  cyanea*)
Mist sprayer
Pebbles
Plastic safari
  animals
Narrow-spouted
  watering can

1 Put some compost (soil mix) in the container, banking it up towards the edges and making a space in the middle for the pool. Scrunch the edges of a piece of foil to make an oval shape.

2 Plunge the houseplants in a bucket of water and wait for the bubbles to stop. Plant the three ribbon plants.

3 Plant the delta maidenhair fern on the other side. Water the bead plant by standing it in a dish of water.

4 The dramatic rosette-shaped dragon tree can go in next. Dragon trees are normally quite tall but this will stay neat and compact.

5 Bead plants are low carpeting species producing bright orange fruits. Dig out a hole and plant it so that it can grow over the edge.

6 To make it feel even more like the lush vegetation surrounding a watering hole, plant a pink quill plant. Add pebbles around the pool to look like boulders.

7 Start to add your plastic safari animals – use whatever African savannah creatures you have. We've put a big elephant at the front but the zebra is hiding in the trees at the back!

8 Carefully fill the pool with water from a beaker. You shouldn't need to water the plants at this stage, but you will need to in future, using a narrow-spouted watering can.

Indoor Pond

If you enjoy growing indoor plants, a mini pond like this will give you a chance to grow some really interesting and unusual types and to look after some pet snails, too!

Pond life

One houseplant that will love spending time in your mini pond is the umbrella plant *Cyperus alternifoli*. It is a relative of the Egyptian papyrus *Cyperus papyrus*, which was used for making paper and reed boats in ancient times.

Below: You can often buy freshwater snails from aquatic or pet stores.

YOU WILL NEED THESE MATERIALS AND TOOLS

Clean washing-up (large plastic) bowl
Small bucket of gravel
Bucket of water
Fibre optic plant (*Scirpus cernuus*)
Parrot feather or watermilfoil (*Myriophyllum aquaticum*)
Canadian pondweed (*Elodea canadensis*)
Water hyacinth (*Eichhornia crassipes*)
Jug (pitcher) of water
Ramshorn or other freshwater snails
Safety scissors

1 Half-fill the washing-up (large plastic) bowl with cold water. Rinse the gravel under an outdoor tap (so the dirt stays outside), then add it to the bowl to form the base of the pond.

2 Plunge the potted water plants in a bucket of water and wait till the bubbles have stopped. This will help them to sink and stay in position. Put the fibre optic plant in one corner.

3 There's no need to take the plastic mesh pot off the plants as they are designed to let the roots grow through. Add the parrot feather.

4 To keep the water healthy, put in an oxygenating plant that lives under the water. Here we are using Canadian pondweed.

5 Squeeze in a small clump of water hyacinth. This strange-looking plant has air-filled bladders that keep the leaves above the water.

6 To help keep your mini pond healthy, add some freshwater snails. They will eat the algae that grows on the walls of the bowl – yum yum!

7 Fill up your mini pond with water, and keep it topped up or the water will disappear through evaporation. Place the pond in a well-lit place, especially in the winter. Cut back overgrown plants with safety scissors.

Beware the invaders!

The parrot feather, Canadian pondweed and water hyacinth plants are all potentially invasive species. They should not be put in outdoor pools where they might "escape".

Birdseed Surprises

"Parrot" and "canary" plants

Packets of birdseed usually contain a mixture of seeds that different birds like to eat. Bigger birds like parrots need bigger seeds while little canaries can only manage tiny ones.

Rebecca and Jock are planting parrot seed in a big pot and canary seed in a smaller one. What will come up and how long will it take to grow? Growing a birdseed surprise garden is quick, easy and lots of fun.

When we grow plants from seed we usually know what to expect because seed packets have pictures on them that tell us what the plants will look like. Sometimes it is fun to grow surprises! Pet stores sell lots of different types of birdseed.

YOU WILL NEED THESE MATERIALS AND TOOLS

Two flowerpots and saucers

Potting compost (soil mix)

Trowel

Two types of birdseed

Compost sieve

Plant labels

Watering can

1 Fill two pots with compost (soil mix) and smooth the surface.

2 Sprinkle the small seed onto the surface of one pot.

3 Cover with a thin layer of sieved compost.

4 Flatten the compost with the base of the other flowerpot.

5 Press the larger seeds into the other flowerpot and smooth the surface. Write a plant label for each pot.

Growing Food for Your Pets

There are lots of different mixtures sold in pet stores, for all sorts of pets. Why not experiment with different types? Hamsters and guinea pigs have some seeds in their food, and they would probably enjoy eating the fresh leaves of the plants you grow. Wild bird food has wheat or barley in it. These seeds will grow into tall grasses with "ears" of corn that you can harvest for pet mice or gerbils.

Below: Watch your birdseed surprises grow into lots of different plants.

6 Water both flowerpots and place them in a warm light place.

Running Up a Bean Pole

Roxy and Dominic are germinating bean seeds and potting them up. The plants curl themselves around bamboo canes so fast that you can almost watch them grow! And they always climb in the same direction – anticlockwise. Measure each day's growth and count how many new leaves appear.

Harvesting your crop
Runner beans need lots of water to make juicy beans. Pick the beans for cooking before they grow too fat because the older ones are tough to eat. Just leave one pod on the plant until it begins to dry out and when you open it you will recognize the big pinky-brown bean seeds that you started off with. Save these to plant next year.

YOU WILL NEED THESE
MATERIALS AND TOOLS

Runner (green) bean seeds

Glass bowl

Watering can

Absorbent cotton and saucer

Peat pots

Compost (soil mix)

Trowel

Big flowerpot

Tall bamboo canes

String or a special cane clip

1 Soak some runner (green) bean seeds overnight in a bowl of water.

2 Make a nest of damp absorbent cotton in the plant saucer. Cover the bean seeds completely, then put them in a warm place to sprout. Check to see that the cotton does not dry out.

3 When the beans have sprouted they can be planted in peat pots. Fill the pots with compost and make a hole. Pop the baby plants in and gently cover the roots with compost.

4 When your plants are 10–15cm (4–6in) tall, it is time to move them to a bigger pot.

5 You can plant three or four in one big pot. Fill the pot with compost leaving at least 5cm (2in) clear at the top. Scoop out a hole for each plant, and gently firm them in place.

6 Your runner bean plants need something to run up, so give each a bamboo cane to climb. Tie them together at the top with string, or use a special clip, and they will grow into a wigwam shape. Your plants will soon be covered in glorious red flowers, which will produce delicious beans, and seeds for next year's crop!

Jolly Geraniums

Geraniums are lovely, bright flowering plants that live outside in the sunny weather. In the winter they can be brought inside to live on a sunny windowsill. Their flowers are either red, white or pink and they have pretty shaped leaves – some of them are scented. Rub a leaf between your fingers to discover their surprising smells of rose, lemon, pineapple or peppermint!

Taking a cutting

The best way to grow your very own geranium plant is to find somebody who owns a nice bushy geranium, and ask them to take a cutting for you. Tania is going to start a plant from a cutting. Just follow the step-by-step instructions, and you will be able to grow one too.

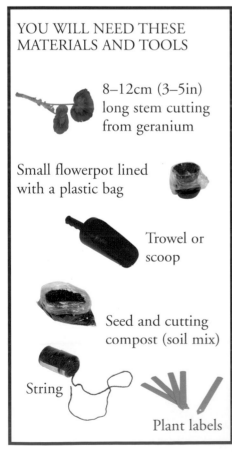

YOU WILL NEED THESE
MATERIALS AND TOOLS

8–12cm (3–5in) long stem cutting from geranium

Small flowerpot lined with a plastic bag

Trowel or scoop

Seed and cutting compost (soil mix)

String

Plant labels

1 Ask a grown-up to take a cutting from a non-flowering shoot of a big geranium plant. Cut the stem just below a node or leaf joint.

2 Take off all leaves except for the small ones at the top.

3 Line a small pot with a plastic bag and fill with moist, but not wet, compost (soil mix). The best type is seed and cutting compost.

4 Make a hole in the compost for your cutting with a finger. Put the cutting in the hole. Press the compost down gently around the cutting to hold it in place.

5 Lift the edges of the plastic bag, gather it up and tie it around the stem of the cutting with string. Take care not to damage the stem by tying it too tightly.

6 Fold the top of the bag back down over the pot, write a label for your plant and place your pot on a light, but not too sunny, windowsill. After ten days your cutting should have rooted. When it has grown new leaves, lift up the plastic bag and you will see new roots in the compost. You can now remove the bag and plant the geranium in a larger pot.

Above: What an achievement – your very own plant from a cutting.

Crazy-Shaped Cress

Once you have learned how to grow mustard and cress (fine curled cress), you can make all sorts of shapes and patterns with your plants. Try animals and faces, or even your own name. Mustard and cress are fun to grow and delicious to eat in salads and sandwiches.

How to grow mustard and cress

Mustard and cress are two of the easiest and quickest plants you can grow. They don't need flowerpots or compost (soil mix), just absorbent cotton and water. Sprinkle the seeds onto damp absorbent cotton and water them each day – as Alex and Reece are doing here. Within a week the little plants will be growing strongly and one week after that you can harvest them with a pair of scissors and then eat them. Your mustard and cress will taste just as good as the type you can buy from supermarkets.

YOU WILL NEED THESE MATERIALS AND TOOLS

Foil dish and roll of absorbent cotton

Watering can

Plastic pastry (cookie) cutter

Mustard seed and cress seed (fine curled cress seeds)

Plastic bag, slightly larger than the dish

1 Line a foil dish with a layer of absorbent cotton.

2 Pour on water, until all the cotton is damp.

3 Place the plastic pastry (cookie) cutter in the middle of the dish.

4 Very carefully, sprinkle mustard seeds inside the cutter.

5 Now sprinkle the cress seeds all around the rest of the dish.

Curly Cress "Eggheads"

You can grow mustard and cress (fine curled cress) in eggshells. Save the shell from your boiled egg and line it with damp absorbent cotton. Sow the seed thickly and wait for your "egghead" to grow its hair. Use felt-tipped pens (magic markers) to draw a happy face on the shell, and trim the mustard and cress into a nice "hair-style".

6 Place the dish in the plastic bag and put it in a dark place. Check the dish each day to see if the seeds have germinated. When they have, remove the plastic bag and place the dish on a light windowsill.

7 Add a little water to the dish each day – just enough to keep the cotton wet. When the plants are as tall as your little finger, you can cut the mustard and cress and put them in a salad or sandwich.

Creepy-Crawly Spider Plants

Spider plants are stripey and spikey and hang down like spiders' legs. They are happy to sit on an inside windowsill or you can put them in special hanging baskets. They will hang down from the ceiling, just like real spiders!

Happy houseplants

In warm countries spider plants grow outdoors, but in cooler places they are mainly grown as houseplants. All they need is some light and water. They will even let you know when they are thirsty, by turning a lighter shade of green. A happy spider plant sends out long stems that have baby plants on the ends, and these can be potted up and grown into new spider plants. Reece will show you how to grow new plants from spider plant runners. Just follow the step-by-step guide here.

YOU WILL NEED THESE
MATERIALS AND TOOLS

Several small flowerpots
and saucers

Trowel

Houseplant compost
(soil mix)

Spider plant
with babies

Hairpins

Watering can

Safety scissors

1 Fill the small flowerpots with compost (soil mix).

2 Press the compost down using the base of another pot.

Other Plants with Babies

The common name of the *Tolmiea menziesii* is the piggyback plant, as new young plants form on the leaves of the parent plant. Just take the leaves with babies on and pin them onto the surface of a pot of compost, using a hairpin. Water and leave in a sunny place. The little plants will soon root and begin to grow. Then you can move them into their own pots.

3 Place the pots around the parent plant, so that a baby plant rests comfortably in each of the pots. Use the hairpins to hold the baby plants firmly in place.

4 Water all the plants. Remember to check the pots each day to make sure that they don't get too dry.

5 When the spider plants have rooted, you will notice new leaves beginning to sprout. Now you can carefully cut the runners.

Right: Finally, the reward for all your care – a new spider plant.

Chocolate-Pot Plant

Can you believe your nose? This lovely plant smells exactly like chocolate! It is a very special sort of cosmos daisy that is bought as a small plant and, if it is kept out of the cold, it will flower again next year.

What a wonderful smell!

To make the smell of chocolate even stronger and more delicious, Dominic and Alex have used a special mulch to cover the soil. This mulch is made from cocoa shells after the cocoa beans have been removed to make chocolate. It has a lovely chocolate smell and is also good for the soil!

YOU WILL NEED THESE MATERIALS AND TOOLS

Large clay pot

Acrylic paint

Paintbrush

Crocks

Cosmos daisy (*Cosmos astrosanguineus*)

All-purpose compost (soil mix)

Trowel

Saucer filled with gravel

Cocoa-shell mulch

Watering can

Right: A chocolate-pot plant would be a lovely and unusual present for someone special – if you can bear to part with it, that is!

1 Use a round paintbrush to paint dots of various bright shades all around your flowerpot.

2 When the paint has dried, put some crocks in the bottom, so that the drainage hole does not clog up.

3 Remove your plant from its pot very carefully. If its roots have started to curl around inside the pot, gently loosen them as Alex is doing here.

4 Put the plant into the decorated pot and fill all around the roots with compost (soil mix), pressing down until the plant is firmly in position.

5 Cover the soil around the chocolate-pot plant with a thick layer of cocoa-shell mulch.

6 Stand the pot on the saucer filled with gravel and water the chocolate-pot plant thoroughly.

7 Press the flower petals gently between your fingers to release a delicious chocolate smell.

8 After all that hard work, and the tempting smells, a real chocolate was irresistible.

More Surprising Smells

A lemon balm plant will grow very quickly. Plant it in a medium-sized flowerpot in all-purpose compost. When you rub the leaves between your fingers, a lovely lemony smell is released. Another surprising plant is one of the sages, *Salvia elegans*. It has a mouthwatering smell of pineapple. There is a mint and a geranium that have a pineapple smell too.

Sprouting Seeds in a Jar

You won't need a garden, or even a windowsill to grow these delicious, crunchy salad sprouts. All you need is a glass jar with some air holes in the lid and some seeds and beans. What could be simpler?

Healthy harvest

If you go to a healthfood shop where they weigh out their own grains and pulses, you will be able to buy small amounts of all kinds of suitable seeds for sprouting. Aduki beans, mung beans, brown lentils, sunflower seeds, chickpeas, sesame seeds and alfalfa seeds are all easy sprouters. You will need to have a jam jar for each type, because every seed germinates at a different speed. A tablespoon of seeds or beans should make about 170g (6oz) sprouts. Laurie and Josie will show you exactly what to do.

YOU WILL NEED THESE MATERIALS AND TOOLS

Jars

Sieve

Chickpeas, mung beans and alfalfa seeds

1 Wash some jars and their lids. You need a separate jar for each type of seed or bean you are using.

2 Ask a grown-up to help you make holes in the lids.

Chinese-Style Beansprouts

The beansprouts that are sold in supermarkets are mung beans that have been germinated in water and kept in the dark. Try growing beansprouts in the same way as salad sprouts, but don't move them into the light. Change their water regularly, and when they look thick and juicy take them out and rinse in a sieve. The beansprouts can be used to make a Chinese stir-fry. Ask a grown-up to mix them up with slivers of carrot, peas, corn and a bit of oil. They only need to cook for 5 minutes. Add a dash of soy sauce for a tasty meal!

3 Put a tablespoonful of seeds or beans in each jar.

4 Rinse the seeds then cover them with lukewarm water.

5 Put the lids on the jars and turn them upside-down, so that most of the water drains away. Put the jars in a warm, dark place for three days.

6 Take them out every morning and evening, and give them a good rinse with cold water, draining each time as in Step 5. After three days, transfer the jars to a warm windowsill, and continue to rinse them out twice a day.

7 When the seeds have roots and leaf-tips they are ready to eat. Empty them into a sieve and rinse once more under the cold tap. Now you have a delicious crunchy salad snack grown in a jam jar!

Vegetable-Top Forest

From roots to shoots

Carrots, parsnips, beetroot (beets), turnips and swedes (rutabaga) are all root vegetables because they grow under the soil. Unless we grow them ourselves, we never see what their leaves look like. But there is a way to grow the leaves from the vegetable tops that we usually throw away. Just stand the top of a root vegetable in a saucer of water, and leaves will begin to sprout from the top!

Rosie and Tania are making up a miniature "forest" using several different vegetable tops. To make it look more realistic they have sprinkled compost and birdseed under their "trees" and grown some undergrowth. Dinosaurs or jungle animals could prowl about, hiding behind trees or sneaking through the long grass!

YOU WILL NEED THESE MATERIALS AND TOOLS

Selection of root vegetable tops

Foil tray

Gravel or small pebbles

Watering can

Compost (soil mix)

Birdseed or grass seed

42

1 Ask a grown-up to cut the tops off a variety of root vegetables for you. Vegetables like kohlrabi, beetroot (beet) and turnips need half of the root, others just the top 3cm (1in).

2 Arrange the vegetable tops quite close together in a foil tray.

3 Surround them with gravel which will look like the forest floor.

Weed Jungle

There is another type of forest that you can grow very quickly – a weed jungle. You have probably heard grown-ups complaining about how fast weeds grow in the garden. They grow even faster if you care for them! Half fill a shallow freezer tray with garden soil or compost. Use a spoon to dig up all sorts of small weeds, and plant them in your tray. Put the tray in a warm place and water when it is dry. Soon you will have a real jungle of leaves and flowers – a perfect home for small model jungle animals.

4 Pour in 1cm (½in) of water and place on a sunny windowsill.

5 Add a little more water each day to make sure the roots don't dry out.

6 When the leaves are about 8cm (3in) tall, sprinkle the compost and birdseed or grass seed over the gravel, and water.

Left: Within a week you will have grown your own vegetable-top forest.

Upside-Down Umbrella Plants

Getting your feet wet

Umbrella plants love water. It is almost impossible to over-water them! This is because they belong to a family of water-loving reeds. They can grow to around 1.3m (4ft) tall and love sharing your bathroom where the air is always humid, and also warm in winter. Try growing them in a glass tank filled with water and pebbles.

Why are they called umbrella plants? Because their stems look like the skeletons of umbrellas. How do they make new plants? Upside down! Have a look at how Joshua and Ilaira are propagating a new plant on the next page, then try it for yourself.

YOU WILL NEED THESE
MATERIALS AND TOOLS

Umbrella plant
(*Cyperus alternifolius*)

Small glass tank

Gravel or small pebbles

Watering can

Safety scissors

Flat-bottomed glass dish

Flowerpot

Trowel

Houseplant compost (soil mix)

1 Take the plant out of its container and stand it in the glass tank, on a bed of gravel.

2 Fill all around the umbrella plant with gravel or stones, to the top of the compost (soil mix).

3 Fill the tank with water to the top of the gravel. Umbrella plants grow naturally in shallow water at the river's edge, and enjoy having wet feet!

4 To make new plants, cut off a flowerhead with 5cm (2in) of stem attached. The flowerheads need to be "mature". If they have brown tufts coming out from their middles they are just right for propagating.

5 Give the leaves a "haircut", so they are about half their original length.

More Water-Loving Plants to Grow

If you have a patio or a garden, you could grow some water-loving plants in a small tub, or washing-up bowl (large plastic bowl). Some plants just float on the water, needing no stones or soil. The water violet is very easy to grow. If you know someone with a garden pond, ask for some small bits from their plants.

6 Fill the flat-bottomed dish with water and float the flowerheads upside-down on the surface.

7 When they have grown some roots, plant them in pots filled with houseplant compost.

Above: A brand new umbrella plant.

Lazy Summer Afternoons

Nasturtiums and pot marigolds are two plants for lazy gardeners! They need very little care – in fact they thrive and produce more flowers in poor-quality soil. So don't pamper them – they just don't like it. Follow the steps shown in the photographs to find out how it's done.

Pretty useful

Nasturtium flowers range from yellow to deep red, and marigold flowers are bright orange or yellow. Nasturtium flowers can be eaten raw. They have a peppery taste, and some supermarkets sell packets of the flowers that would turn a plain salad into a party dish. Marigolds are not eaten but they are used to make soothing skin lotions and healing ointments. Their petals were once used as natural food dyes for cheeses, custards and cakes, too.

Neither of these plants likes to have its roots disturbed, so Dominic and Roxy are starting them off in little peat pots. The plants can be potted on in these because the peat will gradually dissolve into the new compost.

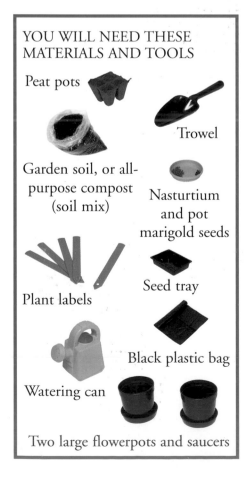

YOU WILL NEED THESE MATERIALS AND TOOLS

Peat pots

Trowel

Garden soil, or all-purpose compost (soil mix)

Nasturtium and pot marigold seeds

Plant labels

Seed tray

Watering can

Black plastic bag

Two large flowerpots and saucers